Life Stories and Legal Histories

Selden Society Lecture
delivered in the Old Hall of Lincoln's Inn
July 4th, 2012
by
WILLIAM CORNISH, C.M.G., Q.C., F.B.A.
*Professor of Law Emeritus
in the University of Cambridge*

LONDON
SELDEN SOCIETY
2015

© Selden Society 2015

ISBN 978 0 85423 225 3

Typeset by Anne Joshua & Associates, Oxford
Printed in Great Britain by
Berforts Information Press, Eynsham, Oxford

LIFE STORIES AND LEGAL HISTORIES

The history of the common law in recent centuries has by now become a thoroughly active field of interest. It was in 1980 that Tony Manchester published his path-breaking *Modern Legal History of England and Wales*; and, in 1984, Gerry Rubin and David Sugarman collected essays by a number of contributors in their *Law, Economy and Society*. These explored the materials and the interpretations, many of them in some sense interdisciplinary, that would come to make up the field. My own contribution, *Law and Society in England, 1750–1950*, was not ready until 1989, partly due to the sad death of my co-author, Geoffrey Clark of University College London, which had occurred as early as 1972. In the last quarter-century, so much ground has been tilled and with such various tools, that the period since 1750 has legal histories, rather than a history. That accounts for the second plural in my title. Courses on modern legal history are becoming available to students in our law schools; and postgraduate research quite frequently involves serious historical assessment, much of it being concerned with the evolutionary processes by which older legal materials were revised and re-moulded to meet the insistent demands of an urbanising society and of commercial, financial and industrial economies – at home, in the Empire and further afield.

The Selden Society is the body preeminent in 'making available to the public' the hidden sources of common law history. So I thought it might be useful to concentrate attention on biography as one of the types of material that contribute to the modern end of that history. Two more specific reasons have attracted my attention to the subject. First, I have recently been involved in placing a collection of legal biographies, made by an old friend, in the Law Department of the London School of Economics, where it is now in the care and development of Professor Linda Mulcahy and Dr Kristen Rundle.[1] It is open for consultation by anyone interested. It still needs additions if it is to measure up fully to the biographical holdings of a few major law libraries. That is the next step for the collection and the Legal Biography Project that is associated with it.[2]

Secondly, my interest was stimulated by the appearance of two essays which have looked at the rise of legal magazines and journals in the nineteenth century, one by David Ibbetson, the other by Stefan Vogenauer.[3] Personal biography is probably the 'next nearest' source to journals. (Indeed when it comes, for instance, to obituaries, there is simply an overlap.[4]) As historians of the book are so actively demonstrating today, by the nineteenth century Britain had a market for literature at many social levels, which was turning bookselling into the distinct activities of publishing and distribution; and among the most popular categories of books were biographies. For, by Dr Johnson's reckoning, 'Biography is, of the various kinds of narrative writing, that which is most eagerly read, and most easily applied to the purposes of life.'[5]

I have chosen the expression, 'life stories', for my title in order to indicate that biographical information of one sort or another is burgeoning in modern legal history and that it may have a great variety of forms: raw documentation such as diaries and letters, lists of basic information about individuals, memorial archives, surveys

---

[1] At the date of publication of this lecture it is in the hands of Professor Mulcahy and Professor Michael Lobban.

[2] Its catalogue can be found at <www.lse.ac.uk/collections/law/projects/legalbiog/lbp-cat1.htm>, accessed August 2014, a useful starting point for anyone wanting to discover biographies that have a bearing on the English legal system in the period from 1850 onwards.

[3] D. Ibbetson, 'English Legal Periodicals, 1829–1870', *Zeitschrift für Neuere Rechtsgeschichte* 28 (2006), pp. 175–194; S. Vogenauer, 'Law Journals in Nineteenth Century England', *Edinburgh Law Review* 12 (2008), pp. 26–50.

[4] Both were part of the phenomenon of publishing as a whole, as its roots spread ineluctably from the invention of the printing press and the ensuing prospects for literary understanding and argument. With improved technologies of printing came the spread of literacy and education; the splay of English language markets across the Empire, America and elsewhere; the ever-increasing divisions of labour at the professional, managerial and commercial levels; the developments of copyright law; and so on.

[5] *The Idler*, no. 84, 14 Nov. 1759.

of surviving material in books and articles. Into the essentially factual, judgements about the individual subject may be admixed, running from the hagiographical to the denunciatory. Some form parts of collections. At one end of these there are biographical dictionaries that stretch from those which add brief summations of the subject's character to the dates, education and offices held (such as, for lawyers, the *Biographical Dictionary of the Common Law*, edited by Brian Simpson in 1984). At the other end come national recordings such as the *Dictionary of National Biography*, edited by Leslie Stephen, and now the *Oxford Dictionary of National Biography*. In between there are publications that include both individual monographs and series of 'lives', such as those of lord chancellors and chief justices, of which the longest remembered, not least for their notoriety, are those written by Lord Campbell, mainly in the 1840s.[6] To them I shall return.

I am not myself a biographer. I cherish those who engage in the absorbing, time-consuming task of writing up a life according to modern standards of historiography. It is splendid to see recent legal history being illuminated by authors, such as two of my *Oxford History of the Laws of England* collaborators:[7] Cocks on Henry Maine,[8] and Smith on Fitzjames Stephen;[9] and beyond them, for instance, Prest on Sir William Blackstone;[10] Melikan on Lord Eldon;[11] Cosgrove on A. V. Dicey;[12] Ford on Lord Brougham;[13]

---

[6] *Lives of the Lord Chancellors and Keepers of the Great Seal of England, from the Earliest Times till the Reign of King George IV*, 7 vols (1845–47); *Lives of Lord Lyndhurst and Lord Brougham* (1868); *Lives of the Chief Justices of England from the Norman Conquest till the Death of Lord Tenterden*, 3 vols (1849–57).

[7] A reference to W. Cornish, S. Anderson, R. Cocks, M. Lobban, P. Polden and K. Smith, *Oxford History of the Laws of England*, vols 11–13, 1820–1914 (Oxford, 2010).

[8] R. C. J. Cocks, *Sir Henry Maine: a Study in Victorian Jurisprudence* (Cambridge, 1988).

[9] K. J. M. Smith, *James Fitzjames Stephen: Portrait of a Victorian Rationalist* (Cambridge, 1988).

[10] W. Prest, *William Blackstone: Law and Letters in the Eighteenth Century* (Oxford, 2008).

[11] R. A. Melikan, *John Scott, Lord Eldon, 1751–1838: the Duty of Loyalty* (Cambridge, 1999).

[12] R. A. Cosgrove, *The Rule of Law: Albert Venn Dicey, Victorian Jurist* (1980).

[13] T. H. Ford, *Henry Brougham and his World: a Biography* (Chichester, 1995), *Chancellor Brougham and his World* (Chichester, 2001).

Duxbury on Sir Frederick Pollock;[14] Lewis on Lord Atkin;[15] and Lacey on Herbert Hart.[16] I am just a legal historian who appreciates the key significance of seeing events, actions and people primarily from the perspective of their own time and within the limits of their own objectives. So I am focusing attention on writing about people while they were still alive or at least within living memory — in a word, *contemporary* biography', as distinct from historical biography which reaches back to earlier times.

With 'contemporary biography', a first division lies between autobiography and writing about others, though the distinction may become blurred, notably when those who have known each other put pen to paper.[17] Those who reflect upon the finest biographies in our literature find a father-figure for the art in Samuel Johnson. Two themes in particular recur in his pronouncements on the subject. The first concerns an innate superiority of autobiography:

> [H]e that records transactions in which himself was engaged, has not only an opportunity of knowing innumerable particulars which escape spectators, but has his natural powers exalted by that ardour which always rises at the remembrance of our own importance, and by which every man is enabled to relate his own actions better than another's.[18]

His second theme is the need to offer judgements on the person as a whole, the bad elements as well as the good — 'warts and all'. As the good Doctor told Boswell: 'If nothing but the bright side of characters should be shown, we should sit down in despondency, and think it utterly impossible to imitate them in *any thing*.'[19] Both

---

[14] N. Duxbury, *Frederick Pollock and the English Juristic Tradition* (Oxford, 2004).
[15] G. Lewis, *Lord Atkin* (1983).
[16] N. Lacey, *A Life of H. L. A. Hart: the Nightmare and the Noble Dream* (Oxford, 2004).
[17] Some dictionary-style records start as autobiography but may become composite, as when *Who's Who* entries are transferred to *Who was Who*. Moreover, if one is in an embracing mood, one might also include as autobiographical those who turn their lives into a form of performance art, such as Caroline Norton, Georgina Weldon, or Henry Brougham.
[18] *The Idler*, no. 104, 14 Nov., 1759.
[19] J. Boswell, *The Life of Samuel Johnson LLD* (1791, G. F. Hill and L. F. Powell, eds (1934–50), iv. 53). Nothing could better illustrate these precepts than

of Johnson's criteria, it should be observed, are directed at content, rather than at literary expression, and that is what makes them significant in assessing the place of biography in a legal history, or for that matter in any history that is broader than a biographical subject per se. So I shall come back to him at the end.

In England, legal biographies – of judges, scholars and lawyers – began to increase in the years when reforms aiming to democratise the parliamentary franchise were set on their century-long haul, paralleled by the establishment of new forms of executive government, central and local. At much the same period, a supreme judicial tribunal for the United Kingdom, the House of Lords, began to assume something of its modern form and significance. Until then its adjudications, occasional though they were in cases from English courts, tended to be reached solely by the lord chancellor of the day, and indeed as the caseload grew, he was for a time formally supported by a revolving rota of lay peers. More significantly, the Lords might summon the judges of the common law courts to express views on the law in a cause, but only by way of advice to the House.[20]

FOUR LORD CHANCELLORS

Within an hour, I cannot survey all the contemporary biographical writing in the nineteenth century about British lawyers or lawmakers. Instead, I shall consider by way of example the personal and professional histories of four men who rose to be lord chancellor in the period 1827 to 1861. My aim is to suggest that knowledge about them from themselves and their contemporaries may add a distinctive measure of explanation to 'legal events' in which they were involved; and accordingly that this biographical material gives the colour of personality to more abstract accounts of

---

the book that first gave Johnson public success: his startling *Account of the Life of Mr Richard Savage* (1744, revised ed. 1748) – poet, playwright, drunkard, debtor – the man with whom Johnson had rambled away from his wife's home for some three years. Much of the book was autobiographical in its reportage and much went to Savage's defects of character.

[20] In *Bright* v. *Hutton* (1852) 3 H.L.C. 341, the same procedure was given an extended scope: see below, n. 53.

the law that record its achievements, its re-directions, its failures. My quartet are: John Singleton Copley, Lord Lyndhurst; Henry, Lord Brougham and Vaux; Edward Sugden, Lord St Leonards; and John, Jock or Jack, Lord Campbell. The extended biographical work given over to them up to Edwardian times is to be found partly in Campbell's *Lives of Lord Chancellors Lyndhurst and Brougham*,[21] which form an addendum to his five earlier volumes on their predecessors; and in the diaries, pamphlets, letters and speeches which each of them, apart from Lyndhurst, would publish in order to set forth his own stance on issues of public importance.[22] To this should be added the lives of contemporary lord chancellors encompassed in the two volumes by J. B. Atlay;[23] the essays on them in Stephen's *Dictionary of National Biography*; and a clutch of further surveys, such as Sir Theodore Martin's *Life of Lyndhurst*,[24] which the Copley family secured two decades after his death by way of antidote to Campbell's highly personal view of what he deemed it fit to record. I shall begin by sketching some of the characteristics

---

[21] For their posthumous publication, see below, n. 30.

[22] Among them, the most profligate was undoubtedly Brougham who resorted constantly to journalism, review articles and more extensive essays, even through his period as chancellor (for an attempt to account for these excursions in a winding biographical narrative, see Ford, *Henry Brougham and his World*; *Chancellor Brougham and his World*). In contrast, Sugden confined his political interventions to occasional, rather stuffy pamphlets, which include the *Misrepresentations,* for which see below, at n. 31.

[23] *The Victorian Chancellors*, 2 vols. (1906, 1908). These include, in volume 1, Lyndhurst (chs 1–7), and Brougham (chs 8–16); and in volume 2, St Leonards (chs 1–2), and Campbell (chs 6–9). For extensive bibliographies concerning each of them, including writing up to the present, see their entries in the *Oxford Dictionary of National Biography*: G. H. Jones, 'Copley, John Singleton, Baron Lyndhurst'; M. Lobban, 'Brougham, Henry Peter, first Baron Brougham and Vaux'; J. S. Getzler, 'Sugden, Edward Burtenshaw, Baron St Leonards'; G. H. Jones and V. Jones, 'Campbell, John, first Baron Campbell of St Andrews'. The judiciary were a popular subject of Victorian admiration, so there was a succession of lesser compilations, of which those that count as 'contemporary' include E. Foss, *The Judges of England*, 9 vols. (1848–64); W. D. I. Foulkes, *A Generation of Judges, by their Reporter* (1886); W. E. Manson, *The Builders of our Law during the Reign of Queen Victoria* (1895), and V. V. Veeder, 'A Century of English Judicature', in *Select Essays in Anglo-American Legal History* (Boston, Mass., 1907), vol. 1, pp. 730–836. See further, P. Polden, in Cornish et al., *Oxford History of the Laws of England*, vol. 11, pp. 959–961.

[24] For which see below, n. 62.

which underlie an attempt to compare their achievements. This will lead me to three specific instances of interactions between them.

The four statesmen-lawyers that I have chosen shared an 'age' in two senses. First of all, they were contemporaries. They were born within a decade of each other, beginning with Lyndhurst in 1772, in colonial America where his father was for the nonce a successful painter of portraits and grand landscapes. They all died at ripe ages: the first, in 1861, being Campbell, while in office as Palmerston's lord chancellor. Lyndhurst died two years later at 91; Brougham in 1868 at all but 90; and finally St Leonards at nearly 94 in 1873.[25] Then there were the 'ages' – the times – through which they shared their lives. The breakaway of the American colonies was fought out while they were children; the wars against the French were *the* national preoccupation of their young maturity. So the 'age' in which they rose to national prominence came after 1815, an age when the effects of industrialisation and the movements into towns and cities were beginning to have extraordinary and disparate effects on the structure of society, the division of labour, and the movement of individuals and indeed of populations. Stirrings of democracy returned to the political forefront from time to time and with it the prospect of reforming institutions of government, including the court system and its judiciary.

Our four, all in their fifties by the 1830s, had already built up prominent careers as advocates and so had considerable wealth and position. Plainly they were ambitious men; and having no solid family inheritance to aid them, they worked with great assiduity and were rewarded for skills that leading barristers provide to clients. The most distinctive among them was probably Sugden, who would climb from being a wigmaker's son to become undisputed leader of the Chancery Bar. He was fascinated from the beginning by that unique complexity, the law of real property and its manifold adjustments in the hands of lord chancellors; and he put his remarkably complete knowledge into law texts, mostly of

---

[25] With his will – famously – no longer locked in its box (though the codicils were still there), nor anywhere else to be found. For which saga see Atlay, *Victorian Chancellors*, ii. 49–52.

massive technicality,[26] though in the end complemented by his *Handy Book*.[27] These were the foundation-stones of his professional success. None of the other three were cut out for such esoteric labour on Sugden's scale. But both Brougham and Campbell engaged in forms of journalism, Brougham as founding figure of the *Edinburgh Review*, Campbell as a reporter of cases at common law and other juridical revelations.

A career at the Bar alone was not in their day enough to reach the heights to which they aspired. They needed a seat in the Commons, procured through 'friendship' with those near the centre of the political groupings that were labelled Whig and Tory. Two of them, Brougham and Campbell, both radicals in youth, turned to the Whigs; and Brougham would use all his energetic vociferousness to become – at least briefly – the great populist of parliamentary reform. On the other side Sugden adhered to the scrupulous conservatism that his great model, Lord Eldon, had personified. And Lyndhurst quickly rubbed off a youthful Jacobin streak when in 1818 he was offered preferment by a Tory government that did not wish to leave so fine an advocate free to appear against it in political trials.[28] In due course, in opposition to electoral reform, Lyndhurst would become a central figure in the Ultra flank of the Tories during the robust confrontations of 1831 to 1832. So there they were, in middle age, divided into pairs in the games of politics.

For each of them, the ultimate measure of success would be to hold the great seal as lord chancellor, a uniquely powerful position in the relations between government and the legal system, which was still rewarded by a range of perquisites, including sinecures for the lord chancellor's family as well as a salary, and then a pension

---

[26] *A Practical Treatise of the Law of Vendors and Purchasers of Estates* (1805), was followed by his *A Practical Treatise on Powers* (1808) and other works. His appreciation of his subject was essentially in Lord Eldon's mode, and indeed Eldon might seek his advice over cases in which Sugden was not engaged as counsel: Atlay, *Victorian Chancellors*, ii. 7.

[27] *A Handy Book on Property Law in a Series of Letters* (Edinburgh, 1858), based on his very first publication, *A Brief Conversation with a Gentleman of Property about to Buy or Sell Lands* (1802).

[28] By 1822 he had become the Crown's solicitor-general.

for life on leaving office. Lyndhurst held the office three times: first as Eldon's successor in 1827, and then twice for Peel: briefly in 1834 to 1835, and for four years from 1841. Brougham was accorded the chancellorship in 1830 because Lord Grey's ministers feared that, left outside their ranks, he might pursue dangerous demands far beyond the limited re-working of Commons constituencies and franchises that they had in mind. Even so, his tenure for four years was enough to convince the core of his party that he remained too demanding and unreliable ever to be let into a Cabinet again. Sugden, taking the title St Leonards, was chancellor only during Lord Derby's short premiership from the spring to the autumn of 1852, having been lord chancellor of Ireland, briefly, for Peel in 1834 to 1835, and then from 1841 to 1845. Campbell, following his long service as a Whig law officer, found himself having to while away the 1840s with his judicial biographies and law reform projects.[29] He was eventually appointed chief justice of the Queen's Bench in 1850. He would only become chancellor nine years later and would die in office in 1861.

That is the briefest of introductions to the careers of my four. I now turn to depict three instances of them in action, which I have chosen in order to show how biography can add its own dimension to the main outline of a legal development. But so as to avoid attaching any undue significance to the biographical element in their conflicts, I have called these instances 'engagements'.

---

[29] Being incurably self-promotional, he drew the attention of Grey, then Melbourne, to his claims for the chancellorship or at least for the mastership of the rolls; but he would end his seven-year term as attorney-general with ennoblement and the lord chancellorship of Ireland, a post that he would occupy for a mere six weeks before Peel and the Tories replaced the Whigs under Melbourne in 1841. In Campbell's place, Sugden went off for his four years in Dublin.

ENGAGEMENTS IN ARGUMENT

Engagement One

My first instance arose during Brougham's lord chancellorship (1830–34), a highly active period to which Campbell would devote nearly a hundred opinionated pages in his *Life of Brougham*. His account, together with his *Life of Lyndhurst*, was written in the 1840s and 1850s but not published until 1869, which was after Campbell himself, Lyndhurst and Brougham were all dead.[30] But the incidents of which I tell concern Brougham and Sugden; and we have them because Sugden was still alive in 1869, and the posthumous appearance of Campbell's *Life of Brougham* caused him to write up his recollection of events with vinegary indignation in a pamphlet entitled *Misrepresentations in Campbell's Lives of Lyndhurst and Brougham corrected by St Leonards* (1869).[31]

During Brougham's chancellorship, Sugden remained leader of the equity Bar that appeared before him. Sugden's well-known protest against Brougham's habit of doing his correspondence (public as well as private) and reading state papers while hearing argument in a Chancery case was an early cause of friction between them. Campbell chose to describe what happened to the 'very petulant but very learned' Sugden as a defeat for him in which he was laughed at by those in court. Sugden, according to his *Misrepresentations*, suffered no such derision. Instead his protest did lead Brougham to behave rather more circumspectly when dealing with letters, government papers and the like.[32] But there were other rubs according to Sugden's account. As part of his determination to reduce the delays in Chancery hearings, Brougham announced that he would resume sitting after the summer recess of 1832 earlier than was usual and Sugden undertook to object to this curtailment of what was, for counsel, a 'necessary holiday'.

In the midst of these controversies, Sugden became 'bugged' by a

---

[30] Hereafter, 'Campbell, *Lives*'.
[31] Published by John Murray; hereafter 'St Leonards, *Misrepresentations*'.
[32] Campbell, *Lives*, pp. 385–386; St Leonards, *Misrepresentations*, pp. 5–9.

belief that Brougham, despite promising legislation to abolish sinecures within his court, was instead filling two vacancies[33] by appointing his favourite brother, James, to them. Being a member of the Commons, Sugden asked an 'innocent' question about who was being appointed.[34] Thereupon Brougham delivered in the House of Lords a highly sarcastic rant against Sugden, which by inference likened him to a maggot or perhaps a horsefly, a taunt that only a few years before might have led to a duel.[35] Brougham's defence of these appointments of his brother was that a person was needed at once to fill the offices, so as to enable the clerks below to carry out the actual registration of court documents. He had chosen James because he could rely on him to resign without claiming

---

[33] One overseeing the Office of Affidavits, the other the Registry of the Court of Chancery. Whether or not properly characterised as 'sinecures', these offices fell vacant upon the death of Robert Scott, whose father, Lord Eldon, had appointed him to them as part of the emoluments of his chancellorship.

[34] *Parliamentary Debates* (3rd) xiv (1832), cols 721–722. That curious Ultra, Sir Charles Wetherell, would praise Sugden for acting in a way that was 'perfectly open, gentlemanlike and honourable', ibid. (cols 818–819). But others thought that Sugden should have made quite sure that notice of his question had been given in advance to the government. Atlay, *Victorian Chancellors*, i. 20–25, stated that Sugden had informed the solicitor-general, Sir William Horne, what he was about to do; but Horne failed to pass the message on to the government. How far this was the true explanation of events remains uncertain.

[35] *The Times*, 27 July 1832, gives a version of Brougham's attack which details the complex rhetoric that he adopted, perhaps to deflect accusations of direct malice against Sugden. The Report of Proceedings (*Parliamentary Debates* (3rd) xiv, cols 738–743, especially at 742) is briefer and less rugged. How *The Times* came by its account is not known (though this was a period when the editor, Barnes, published Brougham's commentaries on other matters); but once he had read it, Peel pronounced the attack so scurrilous that Sugden had every justification for raising it in the Commons (see ibid., cols 833–835). And to this Althorp could reply only that Brougham had called on him to say that he had been misreported, but had provided no account of how (ibid., cols 835–836). Once he had seen the text, Sugden could complain that Brougham had used the soubriquet ten years before to describe the clergy of Durham cathedral (then led by Dr Philpotts, later a controversial bishop of Exeter) when defending a client against a charge of criminal libel; the prosecution had to do with their refusal to toll the traditional peal for the death of a monarch, in that case the unfortunate Queen Caroline. In a pamphlet of 1822 Brougham had reproduced his submissions: see Campbell, *Lives*, pp. 330–332; R. Stewart, *H. B.: The Public Career of Henry Brougham, 1778–1868* (1985), pp. 164–168. The creepy-crawly image may well have come from Alexander Pope's couplet, in his *Epistle from Mr Pope to Dr Arbuthnot* (1735), lines 309–310: 'Yet let me flap this Bug with gilded wings, | This painted Child of Dirt that stinks and stings.'

compensation when he (Henry) put through his promised Act abolishing the 'supervisory' posts.[36]

In his riposte, Brougham provided a stinging example of his habitual ability to combine invective, contempt and 'fun' which had parts of his noble audience cheering him on. Next day in the lower house, Sugden returned twice to the charge, gaining powerful backing from Peel, once he had seen *The Times* report. The issue was then dropped in Parliament, but Brougham seems to have behaved like a sulky child at Chancery proceedings before him when Sugden led for one of the parties. But then he agreed to see Sugden, leaping up from his chair and offering his hand, which Sugden felt obliged to accept. Having succeeded in getting the proposed vacation sittings withdrawn,[37] Sugden announced that he could not live on terms of friendship with Brougham. Brougham was by then already attempting some reconciliation by seeking to offer Sugden a judgeship in the Court of Exchequer. This offer was supposed to have been conveyed to Sugden by Lyndhurst (who had become chief baron in 1830 and had reluctantly agreed to be Brougham's sounding board); but the offer had only been explored, not formally put. Anyway Sugden was in no mood to accept such a side-lining. In the confrontational interview, Brougham directly reiterated his proposal of an Exchequer judgeship as 'a full satisfaction'; but Sugden maintained a frosty silence. Then Brougham suddenly gave in, apparently uttering the memorable line: 'Well, I think when a man feels that he has done wrong,

---

[36] In the Commons next day, Brougham's youngest brother, William, whom he had already appointed a Chancery master, offered this same explanation: *Parliamentary Debates* (3rd) xiv, cols 818–819, 831. The chancellor had assured the Lords that his bill abolishing Chancery offices was already an improved version of one that he had put forward in the previous session. However, its presentation had been delayed so that its content could become part of Brougham's plan to establish a Chancery appeal court. The young George Spence, an M. P. and member of the equity Bar, confirmed this, since he was acting as Brougham's draftsman in the matter (see ibid., cols 818–819). This grander scheme came to nought and the abolition of Chancery sinecures went through on its own with undoubted speed: see below, n. 40.

[37] He argued that the Bar was entitled to its vacation as of right, not by virtue of the chancellor's discretion, which Brougham conceded was 'the true way of putting it' (St Leonards, *Misrepresentations*, pp. 28–29).

the sooner he says so the better',[38] a precept which he had scarcely followed in all the rankling up till then. At which juncture, Sugden shook hands willingly. Indeed, nearly forty years later he would spend much of his complaint against Campbell's *Lives* in insisting that he (Sugden) and Brougham remained friends, rather than enemies, during their long lives.[39] Whatever Brougham may have been up to initially in conferring the sinecure offices on his brother, he did promote the legislation needed to abolish them with all haste before the summer recess in 1832.[40]

So what can we learn from this stormy clash, apparently patched up into an amicable relationship? It is one telling incident in Brougham's rush to muck out the Augean stables of Eldon's Chancery, during which he attempted a great deal more than Lyndhurst had been prepared to shoulder as his predecessor on the woolsack. This charging at so many fences was certainly one aspect of his remarkable character that made him an object of suspicion, not least for the leaders of his own party.[41]

---

[38] See St Leonards, *Misrepresentations*, pp. 28–29. Atlay's verdict on the *Misrepresentations* was that their 'literary composition . . . bears unmistakeable traces of age, and is deficient both in arrangement and in vigour of statement. But as an exposé of Lord Campbell's methods, and of his views as to the obligations of friendship, it is invaluable': *Victorian Chancellors*, ii. 48.

[39] During his short chancellorship in 1852, Sugden would accept mild reforms of Chancery procedure; so he was not by then a diehard resister of Eldon's stamp. Nor had he been an eloquent opponent of reform to the Commons franchise as Lyndhurst had made himself by allying with the elderly duke of Wellington and advising William IV about his constitutional powers: see Atlay, *Victorian Chancellors*, i. 86–99. From the opposite pole Brougham became increasingly conservative; though never exactly a man to trust. In the 1850s Brougham and Campbell were constantly at odds in debate in the Lords: see Harriet Martineau, *Biographical Sketches* (1869), p. 252.

[40] 2 & 3 Will. IV, c. 111. The two offices previously granted to Scott were abolished, as well as ten other posts in Chancery. Even then, Lord Eldon raised a crusty voice against the loss at one swoop of the power to appoint family members to nominal, but remunerative, posts if and when they fell vacant: see *Parliamentary Debates* (3rd) xiv cols 1779–80. However, by section 2 of the Act it was provided that where the current appointee had entered into office before 1 June 1832, it would determine only on his completion of it, thus distinguishing Brougham's appointments of his brother from other cases. Brougham's forthright complaints about the antique remuneration arrangements for the chancellorship were met by a provision in section 3 allowing for a pension to be agreed upon the retirement of a lord chancellor from office.

[41] The reforms of the legal system which he carried through during his

We would probably have known very little about Campbell's determination to portray Brougham in poor light at this inflamed political juncture had he not added enough about Sugden to goad the latter into publishing his own refutation. Campbell had actually contented himself with barbed remarks about Brougham's letter-writing in court; he included nothing about the other issues. It was Sugden who belatedly provided an account of what else had gone on (who knows with what glitches of memory on his own part). From his *Misrepresentations* we can see shifting attitudes to various legal matters: about how, for instance, gentlemen should seek to redress insults and false accusations; about proper procedures for asking parliamentary questions where they implied personal impropriety; about how the chancellorship should no longer be rewarded by such dubious old devices as the power of appointment to sinecure offices; about what a Tory apologist for the existing Chancery thought of Brougham's new-broomery; and about the Whig coterie that would not countenance Brougham in cabinet office again, thus turning him into the exponent of radical legal reforms which drew from him much energetic loquacity but only a trickle of successes, partly because he was left to work from the outside in.

Engagement Two

I move forward twenty years to that decade when the limited liability corporation emerged from its chrysalis, the deed of

---

chancellorship included reducing the backlog of cases pending in Chancery and in the House of Lords, the establishment of the Judicial Committee of the Privy Council and of the Court of Bankruptcy. He also set in train the long process of re-stating and revising English criminal law and procedure; and was much involved in settling the detailed legislation on the new Commons franchise and revision of local government. He failed however in his endeavours to systematise local courts with civil jurisdiction, which would have to wait for the County Courts Act of 1846. His resort to alcohol as a stimulant to parliamentary and juridical outpourings is well enough attested and seems to have been one element in the psychosomatic collapses that he suffered every couple of years. T. H. Ford (in *Chancellor Brougham and his World* (2001)) also blames resort to drugs such as the opiate laudanum, but without showing much by way of hard evidence: on p. 391 alone does the author quote an instance of Brougham acknowledging that he had taken an opiate, in the form of 'Coldnum', when under the weather on a long coach trip. Other references to drug-taking are unsubstantiated assertions.

settlement company. The first statutory intervention of general significance was the Joint Stock Companies Act of 1844, secured by Gladstone (then a Tory minister) as president of the Board of Trade.[42] This Act set up a two-stage system for the formation of companies which involved preliminary registration and final registration, each having its own structures and sets of powers. During preliminary registration, those who supported the venture could be listed as members of a provisional committee. They could be allotted shares as the company began to amass its capital and could then be called upon to pay part or all of the face value of the shares. If the company did not reach final registration or otherwise failed, in winding it up a whole set of issues might arise about the extent of a provisional committee member's liability to creditors, for instance, for the expenses of the promotion. In this there were problems on which the views of judges and other court officers soon began to differ, since a great deal was left without clear definition.[43] A wave of litigation followed.

Hutton v. *Upfill*[44] concerned the winding-up of a company formed to build a railway line from Birmingham to Oxford and further south; but the company got no further than a preliminary registration. Hutton, as a member of the provisional committee, accepted 100 shares for which he was requested to pay a deposit; it being a condition that, if he failed to do so by a given date, the allotment would be nullified. He did not pay this deposit within the time-frame, yet in winding-up proceedings he was listed by a Chancery master as liable to contribute. Who should that master be but Henry Brougham's youngest brother, William.[45] But a

---

[42] 7 & 8 Vict., c.110, together with a Winding Up Act (7 & 8 Vict., c. 111). Soon enough, given the financial turmoil of 1847, the Act needed re-writing twice: see 11 & 12 Vict., c. 45 (1848) and 12 & 13 Vict., c. 108 (1849).

[43] See above, n. 36, below, n. 55.

[44] (1850) 2 H.L.C. 674.

[45] See generally the entry for him in the *Oxford Dictionary of National Biography* (by Lobban). Lord Brougham had appointed William a master in 1831; and had come to hope that William would succeed to his title, an event which did in the end happen, even though it required a special patent excluding the son of their elder brother, John. William adopted something of his brother's penchant for reform by writing a pamphlet (*A Letter to Lord Chancellor Cottenham upon the Bill to give Primary Jurisdiction to the Masters in Ordinary of the High Court of Chancery in*

master's report was not an order of the court, but advice to the judge who ordered it; and Vice-Chancellor Knight-Bruce took the opposite view to Master Brougham: the defendant was not liable to contribute in order to pay creditors involved in the failed formation. The official manager of the winding-up then appealed to the House of Lords. This happened to coincide with a moment when Henry Brougham saw a brief chance to resume some part of his chancellary responsibilities of yester-year. While Cottenham had been chancellor for a second time,[46] much of the decision-making of the judicial House of Lords had been conducted by him; but in 1850 his declining health finally forced him to resign and Brougham was able to decide the appeal in the *Hutton* case 'as the only Law Lord present',[47] overruling Knight-Bruce and restoring the opinion of his brother. He bolstered his judgment by referring to what he said was Cottenham's even more extensive view of the liability of a preliminary committee member.[48]

The root difficulty by this time was that the superior judges of the three common law jurisdictions tended increasingly the other way. Two years later, *Bright* v. *Hutton*[49] reached the Lords. This case

---

Certain Cases (1850)), which associated him with others such as Thomas Pemberton Leigh (afterwards Lord Kingsdown). Their main attack went to the wastefulness of the office of master: see Atlay, *Victorian Chancellors*, i, at 451; E. Heward, *Masters in Ordinary* (Chichester, 1990), ch. 9.

[46] Charles Pepys, at the Chancery Bar second only to Sugden, was appointed chancellor, as Lord Cottenham, by Lord Melbourne in 1836, after a messy few months in which the great seal was placed with three lords commissioners: Pepys as master of the rolls, Shadwell V.-C., and Bosanquet J. There he remained till Peel displaced the Whigs in 1841; and he would return again in 1846–50. Atlay had a good deal to say against him, remarking on his choice of the village of Cottenham in Cambridgeshire for his title as a place 'known to generations of Cantabs as the home of a peculiarly excellent "soft" cheese': *Victorian Chancellors*, i. 394, and ch. 18. For a rounded modern assessment, see F. R. Burns, 'Lord Cottenham and the Court of Chancery', *Journal of Legal History* 24 (2003), 187.

[47] (1850) 2 H.L.C. 674, at 681. He reverted to the earlier practice of having lay peers sit with him; and, as in 1830 to 1834, he was setting about clearing the backlogs that had built up in all the Lords' judicial business (including hearings for parliamentary divorce). His aim, he said, was to allow the lord chancellor (at the time, Thomas Wilde, Lord Truro) to concentrate on Chancery hearings; as to which, see Atlay, *Victorian Chancellors*, i. 415, 450.

[48] (1850) 2 H. L. C., at 694–695.

[49] (1852) 3 H.L.C. 341.

arose out of the liquidation of the same railway project.[50] The principal point of difference from *Upfill's Case* was that here the provisional member not only accepted his allotment of shares but paid the required deposit on them, thereby making it, one would have thought, a stronger case for liability to pay further contributions.[51] This time the 'Law Lords' were in a state of alert.[52] The common law judges having been summoned,[53] St Leonards, who had become chancellor, put the crucial question concerning contribution to liabilities; and they answered that, but for Brougham's *Upfill* decision, which was 'binding on upon every inferior court', they would have held that there was no liability on the provisional member in this case to pay additional calls on the shares. The implication was accordingly that the Lords itself could choose whether to overrule its own earlier precedent. St Leonards seized upon the subtle nature of this answer. Because liability of the defendant in *Upfill* was a mixed question of law and fact, the Lords should leave that decision on one side, 'just where you found it', and the opinion proffered by the judges should be preferred. With this Campbell was ready to agree; and so did Brougham, but with an equivocal admission of defeat. 'The Learned judges have given this opinion. It is not for me to say whether I agree with them or not. It would be superfluous in me to say I agree with them; it

---

[50] In *Law and Politics: the House of Lords as a Judicial Body 1800–1976* (1979), pp. 79–83, R. B. Stevens detects some blurring in the statements of particular judges between *res judicata* questions (whether a court has power to revise an order already given in a particular case), and *stare decisis* questions (whether the ratio decidendi of a Lords decision binds that court as a precedent to be applied in a later case). However, the significance of this difference should not be exaggerated.

[51] In the court below, Lord Cranworth, sitting as vice-chancellor, had considered himself bound to apply *Upfill*, having been informed by counsel that the issue would in any case be appealed to the Lords: see (1852) 3 H.L.C. at 373, 393–394.

[52] As well as Sugden (by then lord chancellor), Brougham, Campbell and Cranworth heard the cause once more. Truro was present for much of the argument but did not speak in judgment.

[53] Other lines of argument led the law lords (on the advice of the judges) to indicate that there was no wider principle of liability in equity than at common law; and to allow questions to be put to the judges as the lords thought fit, whether or not they were raised by the grounds of appeal: see (1852) 3 H.L.C. 341, at 370–372, 380–385 (Bethell Q. C. in argument).

[54] Ibid., p. 390.

would be unbecoming in me to say that I differ from them.'[54]

Of course at issue was that crucial element in the doctrine of *stare decisis*: is a court bound by its own previous decisions, most particularly if that court is the Lords? St Leonards thought that even that tribunal must possess an inherent power to correct an error into which it may previously have fallen.[55] But Campbell, speaking 'with great deference', opined in the name of legal certainty that a rule applied by the House of Lords to a case before it could thereafter be altered only by legislation, a proposition that Lord Halsbury, half a century later in the *London Tramways* case, would claim to have been followed 'for some centuries'.[56] *Bright* v. *Hutton* appears to have been a decidedly unconvincing example of the technique of restrictive distinguishing on the facts. What biography as such adds to anything in the reports of the cases is Campbell's assertion that he was drafting a bill that would reverse Brougham's earlier decision; but 'in order to save Brougham's disgrace . . . we contrived by a little straining and ingenuity in a similar case, to draw distinctions whereby the law on this subject was satisfactorily re-established'.[57] That may have satisfied the Great Biographer; but to us it rather suggests that, while *stare decisis* was the general principle, it could be found to contain subliminal devices for avoiding what the court giving the later decision thought was the wrong line to follow.

---

[55] His position was in line with that of his great predecessor, Eldon, and bore the stamp of a tradition in equity. In the present case the obscurity of the issue was such that, in his view, no judge who, having had to consider the liability of provisional committee members to contribute to winding up, 'had not differed from himself in regard to the points to be decided': (1852) 3 H.L.C. 341, at 389–390.

[56] *London Tramways* v. *London County Council* [1898] A.C. 375, 392. For its history, see Cornish et al., *Oxford History of the Laws of England*, xi., at 50–51, 545–546; cf. Stevens, *Law and Politics*, especially at pp. 88–90.

[57] Campbell, *Lives*, at p. 508. Twenty years before, Brougham had himself promoted a bill to secure the reversal of a court order by Lord Wynford in an appeal to the Lords from Scotland, which contained a plain error of Scots law. Campbell claimed his intended resort to the same tactic as something of a tit-for-tat.

Engagement Three

This takes us on to 1857, when we find the 85-year-old Lyndhurst still in many ways in pole position. Campbell, who had found the 1840s fallow in terms of judicial advancement, had occupied the period not only with the production of serial biography; he had also had taken up the promotion of Acts to modernise the common law in fields such as defamation and fatal accidents. When in 1850 he eventually became chief justice of the Queen's Bench, he had little time for either pursuit. In 1857, however, he presided over a prosecution on indictment for the offence of procuring obscene material for sale, which left him convinced that the country was being besmirched by great effluxes of indecent literature. These must, he decided, be put down at once by new powers of search and seizure which would be given to courts of summary jurisdiction on the complaint of 'any person' (most likely a police superintendent, since by then the new type of police force had to be established in all counties as well as towns and cities). He denounced 'this detestable traffic', claiming that there were 'persons actually employed to travel the country for the purpose of distributing circulars of the most exciting description'.[58]

When his bill came to the Lords on second reading, Brougham and St Leonards were among those who welcomed Campbell's initiative, yet thought that the bill needed substantial amendment.[59] To begin with, there was no definition of obscenity in its text; and secondly the seizure provisions left too great scope for vexatious or revengeful attacks: an ill-intentioned trouble-maker had only to allege to a police officer or other person that there was obscene literature for sale at a particular address for a single magistrate to be empowered to issue a search warrant. But it was Lyndhurst who set about scorching the earth with his opposition. First quoting Dr Johnson's rather cumbrous attempt to define 'obscenity' as 'something immodest, not agreeable to chastity of

---

[58] See the second reading debate in the Lords: 146 *Parliamentary Debates* (4th), cols 327–329 (1857).

[59] Ibid., cols 329, 334. Cranworth L. C. was equally critical: see ibid., cols 329–330.

mind; causing lewd ideas', he employed his special tone of amused disdain to twit Campbell for drafting so vague that it could secure seizure and destruction of publications containing masterpieces of descriptive or dramatic writing, or of pictorial fleshiness; and which would leave decisions about what to seize and destroy to persons of perhaps ordinary station. He adduced a long catalogue of what was likely to be in danger, starting with Corregio's *Jupiter and Antiope*, opposite which, he said, the Louvre placed an ottoman on which ladies of the first rank sat daily in order to study its beauty. He ended by moving that the bill be read six months hence.[60]

At this Campbell apparently lost his temper completely and called Lyndhurst something too despicable to be reported in *Hansard*.[61] At which point, to understand what was going on, we have to turn to biography.[62] When the deaf Lyndhurst was told what the insult was, he refused to receive Campbell at his house in the hope of offering a private apology. However the Lords had by then allowed the bill to proceed,[63] and Campbell had persuaded Lyndhurst to suggest improvements to the drafting, which seems a distinctly thick-necked tactic.[64] At the third reading Campbell did feel obliged to proffer a grudging withdrawal of his earlier remark.[65] This only roused Lyndhurst to renewed anger. He offered an instance of malicious accusation,[66] and reverted to his earlier

---

[60] 146 *Parliamentary Debates* (4th) col. 233 (1857).

[61] The reporter kept his attention on the row over procedure in the chamber which burst forth when Campbell claimed the right to answer Lyndhurst at once, rather than waiting until others wanting to speak had been heard. Some of the cries of 'Order!' in this report, however, may well have gone to Campbell's unparliamentary language about Lyndhurst: 146 *Parliamentary Debates* (4th) cols. 333–338.

[62] See Sir Theodore Martin, *A Life of Lord Lyndhurst from Letters and Papers in Possession of His Family* (1884), pp. 472–475.

[63] Leave of the House was proposed by Brougham: 146 *Parliamentary Debates* (4th) col. 338, and Lyndhurst's objection was withdrawn.

[64] Lyndhurst did comply, in particular by proposing provisions that required the informer to produce evidence for his suspicions; see the records of the committee and report stages in the Lords, when Lyndhurst was not present: 146 *Parliamentary Debates* (4th) cols 864–867.

[65] He maintained that he had said nothing offensive, but excused himself for inadvertence if others might infer something derogatory from his language: ibid., cols 1356–57.

[66] Ibid., col. 1358: the trial, which was on indictment, had been transferred from quarter sessions to the Court of Queen's Bench, such was its importance taken to be.

criticisms by describing Campbell's words as 'more degrading to the utterer than to the person against whom they were uttered'.[67] Perhaps his most cutting thrust was: 'I apprehend that my learned and honourable friend is not always aware of the effect of the expressions that he uses. My noble and learned friend has been so accustomed to relate degrading anecdotes about his predecessors in office that I am afraid that his feelings upon those subjects have become blunted.'[68]

When Campbell's *Life of Lyndhurst* finally appeared there was merely a dismissive reference to their 'rough passage of arms'[69] during the third reading of the Obscene Publications Bill, the episode getting no mention in his diaries.[70] It has been asked whether Lyndhurst's intervention was simply 'senile depravity'. Not at all, said Atlay.[71] Thanks to him the debates rehearsed arguments about double standards that would recur often enough.[72] So in the 1950s, the divisions of opinion were on much the same lines, with more illustrations of high (but frank) literature and art, the publication or exhibition of which might be jeopardised.[73] From them would come the Obscene Publications Act of 1959, with its defence of public good in the interests of science, literature, art, learning, or of other objects of general concern;[74] and the rescue that followed of D. H. Lawrence's *Lady Chatterley's Lover* from any

---

[67] Ibid., col. 1358.

[68] Ibid., col. 1378. He added as an illustration Campbell's presentation to him of a volume which contained paragraphs 'by no means complimentary to myself'. When Campbell's *Lives of Lord Lyndhurst and Lord Brougham* appeared a decade later, it contained more passages of the same character.

[69] See p. 201. His phrase conjures up the discourse over 'manly' ways of reacting to personal insult, without resorting to gunshot, rapier or horsewhip, which was an element in the Sugden–Brougham argument of 1832, already mentioned.

[70] The diaries were published by his daughter; but, as with the *Lives*, this was not until 1870, well after her father's death.

[71] See Atlay, *Victorian Chancellors*, ii. 163–164.

[72] When Campbell's bill reached the Commons in committee, J. A. Rowbuck M. P., following Lyndhurst's example, recited his own list of erogenous classics: 147 *Parliamentary Debates* (4th), cols 1476–77.

[73] N. St John-Stevas did so with relish in his *Obscenity and the Law* (1956).

[74] See section 4, which also specified that experts could give evidence as to the literary, artistic, scientific or other merits of the work.

Index Expurgatorius, which was what Lyndhurst had christened Campbell's objective.[75]

CONCLUSION

By way of conclusion let me return to Dr Johnson and his arguments, the first favouring autobiography for its inner knowledge; the second demanding depictions of individuals that are not just sunny-side up. There is of course room to find the second of these precepts at cross-purposes with the first; but Johnson was looking for measures of potential rather than of achievement. After all, he was ready enough to dismiss the bulk of biographical writing in his day as poor stuff indeed. A century later, it was not just Lyndhurst but many figures of the legal establishment, who condemned Campbell for compounding together an ineffable complacency about himself with snaky commentary on his peers.

I have sought to illustrate how biographical elements can contribute a distinctive measure to legal histories that otherwise concentrate on juridical frameworks and the social and economic justifications for them. I have also suggested that they are likely themselves to be enriching where they can be used to compare individuals who worked together or against each other. Contemporary biography may be found in narratives presented as such (as in the conflicting accounts given by Campbell and St Leonards of the latter's shifting relation with Brougham, which was my first 'engagement'); or as addenda to case law reports (as with the mid-century cases on the liabilities of company formers, which was the subject of my second 'engagement'); or as completion of the picture to be had from, for instance, *Hansard* (as with my third 'engagement' on Campbell's Obscene Publications Bill).

In any case, where the material is contemporary, whether written by the subject himself or herself, or by some other person, there has been some tendency to play down its significance. Those who write biographies of the thoroughly deceased may have to work from 'first

---

[75] 146 *Parliamentary Debates* (4th), col. 332 (1857).

hand' stories, views and attitudes recorded during or soon after the 'life'. Certainly scholars today need to ask themselves how far to engage in deconstructing what was said by the subject and his contemporaries. Even Campbell's biographies of his contemporaries cannot just be dismissed as adding a new terror to death (or indeed to life, as St Leonards had occasion to put it[76]). Campbell sold large numbers of copies, which the cleverest and best-informed read for amusement; but many others for what they took to be true stories.[77] They form part of the political and juristic bombast of their time.

In writing about judicial biography, two distinguished Australian historians, Stuart Macintyre and Wilfrid Prest, have commented recently on the root difficulty for writers not trained in the law of assessing the legal significance of a judge's professional work.[78] Their concern is refreshing, and it is something that those with a legal education also have to wrestle with. In any case lawyers writing histories of judges have to be sensitive in a different way. In their accounts those who handled the business of getting rules into shape in the first place, or of later turning them to other deployments, should show their awareness of the contemporary uncertainties surrounding each move, and of the need to get a contentious legal issue somehow resolved. Those who set out to explore legal results from the past may tend to judge what is settled by the standards and understandings of today, although those certainties may have come about largely through the intervening passage of time.

A sympathetic interest in contemporary biography is not going to provide some prime new revelation in modern legal history. As an historical source it is too full of chance for there to be any likelihood

---

[76] *Misrepresentations*, p. 2.

[77] His lives of past chancellors and chief justices intermingled significant perceptions with inaccurate gossip. Moreover they were sold, for instance, to travellers at railway bookstalls in shilling editions, which might then be challenged by readers with more accurate learning: as in [J. Spedding], *Companion to the Railway Edition of Lord Campbell's Life of Bacon, by a Railway Reader* (1853).

[78] Their comments are part of a series of articles from a symposium on judicial biography contained in the *Adelaide Law Review*, 32,1 and 2 (2011): see S. Macintyre, at p. 7; W. Prest, at p. 185.

of that happening. Who gets written up? By whom? For what readership? But in bringing what it does record more to the fore, biographical emphasis gives immediacy to the background of legal change. That is why researchers moving into the legal history of the recent past should spot controversies, amusements, contradictions and expectations in such material. To be on the lookout for these things should be part of their historical journey from early on in their endeavours.

THE SELDEN SOCIETY

The Society was founded in 1887 'to encourage the study and advance the knowledge of the history of English Law'. It publishes annual volumes of source materials such as law reports, court records and other kinds of professional literature. In each case the text is provided with a translation (when the original is in Latin or French) and with full indexes and other apparatus. The introductions to these volumes comprise a substantial proportion of the research done in modern times on the history of the common law; and they and the materials themselves are important for social, economic, constitutional, and linguistic historians, and also for students of local and family history. The Society has in fact averaged a little more than a volume a year; and 2015 will see the publication of the 132nd volume in the series.

There are now about 1,600 members in some 30 countries, mainly the United Kingdom, the United States and the Commonwealth. These members include, in addition to legal historians, professional and amateur, many distinguished judges and practising lawyers, together with most of the major university, court and official libraries in the English-speaking world.

The Society's work and publications programme depend almost entirely on the income it receives by way of members' subscriptions. It has therefore constantly to try to increase its membership to keep pace with mounting costs. The annual subscription for individual members is £30 (U.K.), $65 (N. America) and £35 (all other countries). For institutions, such as libraries, courts and law firms, the rates are £40, $90 and £45, respectively. For this subscription a member receives without further charge the annual volume, the annual report of the Council of the Society and occasional literature, including published lectures such as this; and is entitled to special concessional rates on other publications. Anyone who would like further information may obtain it from the Secretary, Selden Society, Laws Building, Queen Mary, Mile End Road, London, E1 4NS (020-7882-3968; Fax: 020-7882-7636; Selden-Society@qmul.ac.uk).

RECENT SELDEN SOCIETY LECTURES

1981   THE NATURE OF BLACKSTONE'S ACHIEVEMENT
S. F. C. Milsom, F.B.A., Fellow of St. John's College and Professor of English Law, University of Cambridge, Literary Director of the Selden Society.

1983   CANON LAW AND ENGLISH COMMON LAW
R. H. Helmholz, Professor of Law, University of Chicago.

1986   WHY THE HISTORY OF CANON LAW IS NOT WRITTEN
Charles Donahue Jr., Professor of Law, Harvard Law School.

1990   THE THIRD UNIVERSITY OF ENGLAND: THE INNS OF COURT AND THE COMMON-LAW TRADITION
J. H. Baker, F.B.A., Professor of English Legal History, University of Cambridge, Literary Director of the Selden Society.

1995   VICTORIAN LAW AND THE INDUSTRIAL SPIRIT
A. W. B. Simpson, F.B.A.

1999   OBSERVING AND RECORDING THE MEDIEVAL BAR AND BENCH AT WORK: THE ORIGINS OF LAW REPORTING IN ENGLAND
Paul Brand, F.B.A., Fellow of All Souls College, Oxford.

2000   COMMON LAW AND JUS COMMUNE
David Ibbetson, Regius Professor of Civil Law, University of Cambridge.

2001   LAWYERS AND THE STATE: THE VARIETIES OF LEGAL HISTORY
Patrick Wormald, Student of Christ Church, Oxford.

2004   THE VARIED LIFE OF THE SELF-INFORMING JURY
James Oldham, St Thomas More Professor of Law and Legal History, Georgetown University.

2005   LEGAL EDUCATION IN LONDON 1250–1850
Sir John Baker, Q.C., LL.D., F.B.A., Downing Professor of the Laws of England, University of Cambridge.

2006   F. W. MAITLAND AND THE ENGLISHNESS OF ENGLISH LAW
J. G. H. Hudson, Professor of Legal History, University of St Andrews.

2007   BLACKSTONE AS A BARRISTER
Wilfrid Prest, Professor of Law, University of Adelaide.

2008   THE WELSH LEGAL TRIADS
Sara Elin Roberts

2009   COLLECTING ENGLISH LEGAL MANUSCRIPTS
Anthony Taussig, of Gray's Inn and Lincoln's Inn, barrister.

2010 JOHN SELDEN AND THE NORMAN CONQUEST
George Garnett, Fellow of St Hugh's College, Oxford.

2011 THE ORIGINS OF THE ENGLISH PARLIAMENT
John Maddicott, F.B.A., Fellow of Exeter College, Oxford.

2012 LIFE STORIES AND LEGAL HISTORIES
William Cornish, C.M.G., Q.C., F.B.A., Professor of Law Emeritus, University of Cambridge

2013 DOUBLE TROUBLE: THE RISE AND FALL OF THE CRIME OF BIGAMY
Rebecca Probert, Professor of Law, University of Warwick